THE KNOPF POETRY SERIES

HUNDREDS OF
FIREFLIES

HUNDREDS OF FIREFLIES

P O E M S B Y

BRAD LEITHAUSER

ALFRED A. KNOPF   NEW YORK   1982

This Is a Borzoi Book
Published by Alfred A. Knopf, Inc.

Acknowledgments: "Hundreds of Fireflies," "The Return to a Cabin," "A Michigan Ghosttown" and "Angel" originally appeared in *The New Republic*; "Alternate Landscape," "Canoeing at Night," "Dead Elms by a River" and "Along Lake Michigan" in *Poetry*; "The Ghost of a Ghost" and "Old Hat" in *The Kenyon Review*; "11 Astronomical Riddles" and the second part of "Two Summer Jobs" in *New England Review*; "A Quilled Quilt, a Needle Bed" (under the title "A Needle Bed") in *The Atlantic Monthly*; the first part of "Two Summer Jobs" in *Book Digest*; "Daybreak" in *Harvard Magazine*; "Giant Tortoise" in *Heatherstone Review*; "An Expanded Want Ad" in *The New Yorker*; "Additional Bats" *Partisan Review*.

Author's note: "11 Astronomical Riddles" is dedicated to David Mohney, "Two Summer Jobs" to John Chapman, "Daybreak" to George McMillan, "An Expanded Want Ad" to Ann Hulbert, "Giant Tortoise" to Amy Clampitt, "Angel" to Carolyn Cyran, "Birches" to Priscilla Johnson McMillan, "Minims" to Richard Lyon, "Canoeing at Night" to John and Stan Nevin, "The Ghost of a Ghost" to Rick Nevin, "The Return to a Cabin" to my brothers, Neil, Mark and Lance Leithauser, and "Hundreds of Fireflies" to my wife, Mary Jo Salter. I am especially grateful to The Mary Roberts Rinehart foundation; to Daryl Hine, the first editor to publish any of my poems; to Ann Close, for patient and thoughtful assistance throughout; and to Anthony Hecht, for his characteristically bountiful kindness and encouragement.

LIBRARY OF CONGRESS CATALOGING IN PUBLICATION DATA

Leithauser, Brad.
Hundreds of fireflies.

(Knopf poetry series; #6)
I. Title
PS3562.E4623H8   1982   811'.54   81-47481
ISBN 0-394-51949-3   AACR2
ISBN 0-394-74896-4 (pbk.)

Manufactured in the United States of America
First Edition

To My Parents With Love
Gladys Garner Leithauser
and
Harold Edward Leithauser

So he who strongly feels,
behaves. The very bird
   grown taller as he sings, steels
his form straight up. Though he is captive,
his mighty singing
says, satisfaction is a lowly
thing, how pure a thing is joy.

"What Are Years?"
MARIANNE MOORE

CONTENTS

HUNDREDS OF
FIREFLIES

AN EXPANDED WANT AD

Rent—cttge Pig Riv
3 bdrm stove fridge
20 acr—lovely view

Although it's true
a few screens are torn and various
uninvited types may flutter through,
   some of them to bite you,

   and true the floors
buckle and sag like a garden plowed
by moles, which makes the shaky chairs
   seem shakier, and the bedroom doors

   refuse to close
(you'll have three bright bedrooms—and a fine
kitchen, a living room with fireplace,
   and bath with shower hose),

   there's a good view
of the Pigeon, a river that carries
more than its share of sunny jewelry,
   for days here are mostly blue,

   and nights so clear
and deep that in a roadside puddle
you can spot the wobbly flashlight flare
   of even a minuscule star.

The jolting road,
two muddy ruts, flanks a weedy fan
that slithers against the underside
of a car, then rises unbowed,

but better still,
go on foot—though this means mosquitoes—
and stop at the overgrown sawmill,
with its fragrant wood-chip pile,

and, stooping, enter
that shack the length of a compact car
where two loggers outbraved the bitter
sting of a Michigan winter.

The room is dim,
spider-strung; you'll sense the whittled lives
they led—how plain, pure, and coldly grim
the long months were to them . . .

Just a short ways
up the road you'll come to a birch clump
which on all overcast mornings glows
with a cumulus whiteness

and in the brief
light after sunset holds a comely
allusive blush—a mix that's one half
modesty, the other mischief.

While if you hike
to where the road feeds a wider road
you'll find a mailbox above a choke
    of weeds, leaning on its stake;

    it looks disowned,
worthless, but will keep your letters dry
though its broken door trails to the ground
    like the tongue of a panting hound.

    Venture across
this wider road to reach a pasture,
whose three horses confirm that "the grass
    is always greener" applies

    to them as well:
offered shoots from your side of the fence,
they'll joggle forward to inhale
    a verdant airy handful,

    and will emit
low shivering snorts of joy, and will—
while you feed them—show no appetite
    for the grass growing at their feet.

    Now, it may happen
the first nights you'll feel an odd unease,
not lessened by the moths' crazed tapping
    at the glass; and later, sleeping

unsteadily,
as bullfrogs hurl harsh gravelly notes
from slingshot throats, you may wonder why
   you ever left the city.

   Should this occur,
think of the creatures you've not yet glimpsed,
the owl and woodchuck and tense-necked deer
   you'll meet if you remain here;

   remember, too,
morning's flashy gift—for when day breaks
it mends all wrongs by offering you
   drenched fields, nearly drowned in dew.

ALTERNATE LANDSCAPE

I

In some heavy clouds our flight
was a passage through blindness,
but everything white, not dark.
Their dense centers were strangely
turbulent; the wings rattled
as we rose to a brilliance,
    whiter yet, into the clear.

II

And there space: a chill expanse
widening out, a fluent
surface breaking in the light.
Inflated shapes suggested
maps or faces; maybe scrubbed
knobby heads of cauliflower,
    or clusters of white balloons.

III

Too cold, too thin here even
for birds; yet this pale country
dips, surges, as if alive
reels to the push of bright light.

Mountains roll slowly downhill;
huge piled waves threaten to break,
then collapse upon themselves.

IV

Below, where clouds turn sheer, shades
of colors slip through a mist,
almost clear, like a river
under a fine skin of ice:
another life, rushing past—
until snowdrifts fill the gap,
and all the colors are lost.

V

Clouds with firm edges, held by
stormy centers, spin their forms
under a perpetual flash,
grease-fire ring of light: sun far
too bright, another blindness,
burns through uncluttered distance
from a high place without clouds.

MINIATURE

Beneath lilac clusters on a plain
two feet by two, two
long-necked dandelions sway
over a toiling community;
grain by grain,

coppery skin
blazing as if sweat-painted,
the ants amass a sort of pyramid
on Mayan lines: broad
base and truncated cone.

One dandelion
is yellow, is a solar flame
spoking from a green nether rim;
the other gray, a dainty crumb-
cake of a moon.

Soon gusts will shake
this moon and it—no moon at all—
detach a drifting astral
scatter; no sun, the sun cool
and blanch and wear a lunar look;

but under weighted air, noon's
dominion, laborers erect a temple
to this sun and moon, unable
to compass decay, indeed unmindful
of all suns and moons.

Binoculars I'd meant for birds
catch instead, and place an arm's length away,
  a frog
compactly perched on a log that lies
  half in, half out of the river.

He may be preying, tongue wound to strike,
but to judge from his look of grave languor
  he seems
to be sunning merely. His skin gleams with light
  coming, rebuffed, off the water; his back's

tawny-spotted, like an elderly hand,
but flank's the crisp, projecting green
  of new
leafage, as if what ran through his veins
  was chlorophyll and he'd

tapped that vegetal sorcery
which, making light of physical bounds,
  makes food
of light. Given the amplitude of his
  special greenness, it requires no large hop

of imagination to see him as
the downed trunk's surviving outlet, from which,
  perhaps,
dragged-out years of collapsing roots
  may prove reversible. With a reflection-

shattering *plop,* a momentary
outbreak of topical, enlarging rings
      that chase
one another frenziedly, the place's spell
    is lifted: the trunk bare, the frog elsewhere.

HUNDREDS OF FIREFLIES

Sky yet violet,
shadows collecting
under the trees

and first stars wan
as night birches, the fireflies
begin: from the first,

the night belongs
to them.
        Darkness brightens
them: from our screened porch

we watch their blinkings
sharpen: three, four of them
lighten nightfall of all

solemnity; ten or twelve
and the eyes are led
endlessly astray;

and in deeper night
it's twenty, fifty, more—a number
beyond simple reckoning—

and still they keep
coming.
          No winter
surpasses the flash

of their storm, no spring
their startling growth.
                    Expanding
to contain them, the night fills

with their soundless poppings,
hundreds of fireflies,
each arhythmic light a trinket

to entice some wayward mate
into the joined darkness
of propagation . . .

So it's as wooers they come
bumbling to the cottage screens
to illumine palely, eerily

our faces, and but a creature's
prime, combinatory urge
erects constellations brighter,

nearer than the heavens
will ever be.
                    Merely
to watch, and say nothing,

gratefully,
is what is best, is
what we needed.
                    For we've seen

stars enough tonight
to hold us through a year
of city living—

14

lengthening fall nights,
opened trees and the rosy
murk of shopping plazas;

and skies grayly gathering snow,
and the moon of crusted snow,
and marshy April skies clogged

with sediment . . . until the silent
drift of summer through the trees
signals us, drawn too by light,

to another brief firefly season.

A QUILLED QUILT, A NEEDLE BED

Under the longleaf pines
The curved, foot-long needles have
Woven a thatchwork quilt—threads,
Not patches, windfall millions
Looped and overlapped to make
The softest of needle beds.

The day's turned hot, the air
Coiling around the always
Cool scent of pine. As if lit
From below, a radiance
Milder yet more clement than
The sun's, the forest-carpet

Glows. It's a kind of pelt:
Thick as a bear's, tawny like
A bobcat's, more wonderful
Than both—a maize labyrinth
Spiraling down through tiny
Chinks to a caked, vegetal

Ferment where the needles
Crumble and blacken. And still
The mazing continues . . . whorls
Within whorls, the downscaling
Yet-perfect intricacies
Of lichens, seeds and crystals.

ODD CARNIVORES

A Venus Flytrap

The humming fly is turned to carrion.
This vegetable's no vegetarian.

A Mosquito

The lady whines, then dines; is slapped and killed;
yet it's her killer's blood that has been spilled.

i. The Sun

I am a blinding eye.
I will never relent.
I am magnificent.

I dare them to try.
They hide in the black.
Afraid to attack.

ii. Mercury

I huddle closest to the heat
Yet my back is cold
As ice. I am the most fleet,
If the least bold.

iii. Venus

I am tempestuous, hot and cloudy.
I pay no mind.
Love was intended to be rowdy,
Torrid and blind.

iv. Earth's Moon

I'm an aging beauty, unique because
It is night not day that betrays my flaws.

v. Earth

I am the spry little
Cell. I am the riddle
Of the chicken or the egg, the miracle of birth.
But for me, none in the heavens would have any worth.

vi. Mars

Chill, frail, friendly . . . I've been misunderstood:
My color shows a love of warmth, not blood.

vii. Jupiter

The vastest and best am I, the eldest son.
Son in one sense if not the other one . . .
Yet I will be king when his day is done.

viii. An Asteroid

Small, I turn with the great. I feel the same
Call of gravity, though I have no name.

ix. Saturn

Too pretty a ring steals praise from its hand,
Unless the hand be fair enough to wear it.

Around my throat I hook an ivory band.
True beauty is bold; I know my own merit.

x. Uranus and Neptune

We're twins, big-boned boys, pale and overweight.
You mustn't criticize us if we're late.
    It's hard for us to run.
A single lap is an enormous length.
We try not to think, to conserve our strength.
    Sleeping is the most fun.

xi. Pluto

All the others look in; I out.
All the others believe; I doubt.
I stand at the gate of unending Night,
   My fingers on the handle.
Who, when they could have uncountable Light,
   Would settle for a candle?

CANOEING AT NIGHT

I

Water pulled on wood at first
And muscles bunched. We struck
The bank once, with dull solidity.
Spinning free, we turned a wide arc,
Sliding through forest into forest,
Changes that brought no change. Cold,
Cramping, we wanted more than this.
We worked against ourselves,
Shoveling up water that dropped away,
Digging holes in the river
That filled behind us.
We thought of the lamp
Hung downstream on a limb.
Stop, it meant, and that
Is what we wanted.

II

Later we get our timing back.
Clapping bats come down to us,
Sounding us out. And though
Not quite sure of the river,
We steer for the center
And catch the cold drift of it.
We wait for something: a snapping
Of fish, a rustling in the grass;

We wait to face a silver animal
Rapt in its own reflection.
Listening straight into the woods,
We try to lose all other
Noises—the wrinkling of water
Or our own steady breathing.

III

Here, the river is deeper. The moon
Climbs up over the woods. We move
Fast, and in this new light
It is all white water.
Smoothly opening up to us,
The river falls forward;
Trees swing by, bobbing,
As if they float on water.
You and I, we take the bends together,
One good turn on another, moving
Along to where our knot of light
Lies unraveled in the water.

The moon by mid-morning has
the familiar yet neglected face
of a broken clock.

Big, vacant egg. Or a curled late
sleeper. Or a dusty plate.

At this hour, it seems the plug
or stopper in a colossal tub
of tinted water.

Sea-sweat, and tide tugger. Or dry stone-
tip in a river, bleached to bone.

It tarries in the day's path,
frail as a spot of breath
on a windowpane.

O-curving cloud. Last of a few.
Wan reminder of the black behind the blue.

ADDITIONAL BATS

Nightfall loosens them from the rocks
  And trees to which like mushrooms
They fasten. Against the clearing's still-
  lavender sky, dissolving in

And out of sight as fish will
  Under the glinting and smoky
Lid of a stream, the bats
  Pull to their swarm additional bats.

Theirs seems a gimpy flight, crude
  Aerial gallop, yet they live
By hunting on the wing—swoop to strain
  The quick night air for food—

As an outflung vision, surer
  Far than sight, sounds the treetops
At clearing's edge, the outcrops
  Of stone, the ferns, the dense, standing

Water in the overhung ditch,
  And returns as rumpled echoes to
Ears that map the field according to
  Its shifting, imperfect pitch.

GIANT TORTOISE

Suggests a gift
for guessing weather: the big club-head
on its extensible neck, swaying
as if to read the shift
   of patterns overhead.

   Never glimpsed his own patterned back,
the stucco clustered pigments there.
But carried it everywhere,
a lived-in relic: calendar stone
   with muddy undeciphered zodiac.

   Like dried mud, hide's netted
with cracks. The uneven jaws
rarely close. No teeth, but claws
of dusty lumps of quartz,
   centuries old, like all his parts.

   Older than whales,
elephants, even some
tall forests, and grown secure
in an arrived-at wisdom:
   only the self-contained at last endure.

   No memories. What last are appetites only:
the prickling fluids
that spin through him thinly,
immediate, but remotely felt—
   like rain tapping the back of his shell.

THE RETURN TO A CABIN

Cool suddenly,
your first night, and so queer
at once to discover

how many things
you'd forgotten or concealed:
the forest thickening and the wild

frantic ticking in the weeds
like a thousand racing clocks
and the loose packs

of what could be birds
gathering over the river but
for their peculiar, skidding flight;

in a spare, wooden room
that seems with the nightfall
to have changed its smell

you move and even think
warily, new noises sinking in
by way of your prickled skin . . .

You retained the joys
of a sunset here — cloud
and birch-clump dyed

the same watery pink
and the day's last light
bundled off by the river—but not

the succeeding fright
which catches like a burr
in the chest, threatening to tear,

and nothing of how a sky
so overrun by stars
can chase a person indoors

and nothing of the frenzied
strength of moths—just like a man's
knock—knocking on the windowpanes.

TWO SUMMER JOBS

I. Tennis Instructor, 1971

Transformed: the high school graduate, now
himself a teacher for the city.
Not sure who my students are, or how
exactly a tennis class is run,
I show up an hour ahead of time.
Odd: nobody here. But one by one
they appear and—and they're all women!
Maddeningly shy, the truth is I'm
more alarmed than pleased at this, although
a number of them are pretty,
and one, Mrs. Shores, extremely so.

Mine's a small yet adequate domain.
Three mornings a week I hold court
on two courts beside the railroad track—
giving, to those I can, assistance,
and verbally patting on the back
the irretrievably maladroit
whose shots are always rocketing
the fence. Occasionally a train
hurtling to or from Detroit
rumbles through, erasing everything
before it fades into the distance.

Distant but surreally vast,
exclusive, quick to take offense,
the "Big H," Harvard, which only last
April accepted me, now conspires
(my latest crazy daydream runs)
to bar me from settling in a dorm
because I typed "No class presidents,
please" on my roommate selection form.
Just as I'm lunging toward the ball,
a sniping voice within inquires,
"What will happen in the fall?"

The days are changeless, but the weeks pass,
edging me closer to fall, and school.
Mrs. Shores, the day of our last class,
gives a party on her patio,
where I'm handed a glass-bottom mug
—surprise!—engraved with my name.
Beer's offered; I'm too proud to confess
I hate the stuff. It's hot as a blow-
torch now, and not yet noon. The first slug
of Stroh's goes down in a cool
wash of cleansing bitterness.

The party warms up, visibly. Ice
crackles in the drinks. I'm nonplussed
when Mrs. Binstock unfolds a tale
which—though nothing you shouldn't say
among men—is not exactly nice.
My face, which lets me down without fail
at such times, blushes. They laugh at me.
Then, and this is odd, I am discussed
in a fond but distant-seeming way,
as if I were no longer here.
The ghost accepts another beer.

Mrs. Dow speaks of a friend's friend's son
who committed suicide after
his first Harvard exam. A lighter
flares beside me, and cigarette smoke
crowds the air. "Teacher don't allow
any smoking." Freshened laughter
greets sad Mrs. Klein's unlikely quip.
Then, from Mrs. Shores: "What kind of writer
do you want to be?" How, how, how
did she ever draw from me my one
most private wish? I'm tempted to joke,

but a stilled politeness in the air
and the depths of her dark handsome eyes
forbid it. Yet when I stumblingly
begin a pained, self-conscious reply
she is mercifully there
to cut me off; conversation drifts
lightly away, as once more I
find myself taking shelter in
something that soothes as it puzzles me—
a solicitude that's graceful, wise,
and impenetrably feminine.

I drain my mug. A white film adheres
to the glass bottom, and then bursts:
disclosing these my students seated
around me in the Michigan sun,
the last of our lessons completed.
Wobbly I rise, drunk with success
(successfully having drunk four beers!),
and wave goodbye—but forget the press
to my racket. I'm called back amid
much laughter. Once more I gravely bid
them all farewell: So long. It's been fun.

... And what a day this is! The air
humming in my ears, the sun stroking
overheads in the treetops! Now
a second film breaks, revealing how
the light-drinking leaves, the houses, cars,
power lines, a peeling wooden fence
and the pavement's constellated stars
are a network, supple and immense,
and all linked to distant Mrs. Shores,
who calls—but surely she is joking—
"Never forget: the world is yours."

II. Law Clerk, 1979

My fingers having checked and re-checked my tie,
I'm at ease—or nearly so. We're lunching high
over Manhattan, a hundred floors above
streets new to me still. He asks whether I

find the work "exciting." Behind him a buffet
tastefully boasting shrimp, squid salad, paté,
beef, chicken, cheeses, and some good marinated
mushrooms, calls me to come boyishly away

and fill my plate a second time. And I'd love
another beer. I think he thinks that one's enough.
"Exciting? Very"—which is not untrue.
"Best of all"—I'm speaking off the (starchy) cuff—

"I liked the document search in Tennessee."
Indeed, I did. How strange, how fine to be
a someone someone flies a thousand miles
to analyze ancient business files! Now he—

but who is he? A *partner,* first of all,
by which is meant no confederate or pal
of mine, but a star in the firm's firmament.
He's kind, though, funny, and lunch is going well

enough—the conversation light, the view vast
beyond my farthest hopes. The kid's arrived at last:
not just New York, but New York at the top.
Just think of all the noontime views that passed

into the void because I wasn't here! Think
of the elevated wines I never drank
in this very room! The tortes I failed to eat!
—Lunch here is money in the memory bank.

Why, then, wishing I were somewhere else? Why
does my glance drift sidelongingly, my mind stray
from his fatherly banter? When will I shake
this shakiness? It's worse at night. I sometimes stay

late at the office. The place starts thinning out
by six; cleaning women, outfitted to fight
their bosses' daily disarray, marshal vacuums,
trashbins, brooms. Their leaving leaves me free to write,

or to try, as the city underfoot
starts breathing visibly, bubbles of light,
hundreds and hundreds, a champagne glitter
promising love and—more—a distant, delicate

loveliness. *Here* is inspiration. Yet the clock
clicks; my mind does not. Could this be "writer's block,"
nothing but that ailment which, like tennis elbow,
raises its victim's status? Yet it's no joke,

this scooped-out feeling, a sense that language
will never span the gap within. The Brooklyn Bridge,
trafficking in cars and literary ghosts,
shimmers mockingly below. I can't budge

the block; thwarted, I inch instead toward parody,
Keats' "On the Grasshopper and Cricket" to be
wittily urbanized as "The Snowplow
and the Lawnmower"; I'll set "The poetry

of earth is never dead" upon its head.
And yet, though I have the title, and the thread
of a joke as a starter's cord, "Snowplow" will not
start: some mechanical failure under the hood.

In a later, hopeless project Shakespeare
writes in a fancy bar — "To beer or not to beer"
and "The Singapore Slings and Sombreros
cost an outrageous fortune." I'm going nowhere . . .

Most nights, the air's sticky. Too hot to jog,
I take myself out for a walk, like a dog,
once round the block. Inside, endlessly, my
electric fan rustles like a paper bag;

and armed with a borrowed book called *Parodies,*
I rifle my old English 10 anthologies
in search of targets. It seemed this would be simple
but it's not. And I'm hot. And the nights pass

slowly. Then: a new month: still stuck, parodies lost,
when, wolfing lamb at lunch, I find I've crossed
Cinderella's fable (a cleaning woman swept
like me into moneyed worlds) with — Robert Frost.

"Whose shoe this is I need to know.
Throughout the countryside I'll go
In search of one whose gaze is clear,
Whose royal skin is white as snow."

Now *this* is simple, stanzas dropping into place,
and while I couldn't say precisely what it is
I'd like to say, just writing quickly is enough.
And the last stanza is, I think, quite nice:

"And if she's lost, I'll settle cheap—
A helpmate from the common heap,
Some kitchenmaid or chimneysweep,
Some kitchenmaid or chimneysweep."

What now?—next? Will the impasse pass? After work,
I'm roundabouting home through Central Park
when a voice cuts short all questions. *"Bradford."*
It sounds like someone I hope it isn't. ". . . Mark."

He's wearing jeans and a work-shirt with a rip
in the neck, whereas I'm caught in the trap-
pings of a Wall Street lawyer. As we lob our
pleasantries across the Sartorial Gap

he studies me. Mark's a poet too, if you take
the thought for the deed—but who am I to talk?
At Harvard, hardly friends, we were nonetheless
drawn together by a fiercely sophomoric

contest: my-potential's-bigger-than-yours.
He's just in for the day, he quickly offers,
as if this were a kind of feat. City living
taints the artist's soul—he's suggesting of course—

which is his old, still tiresome refrain. So why
do I yet feel some need to justify
myself to him, who, he tells me, moved to a farm,
makes pots (a bad sign) and (I'm sure) lives high

on Daddy's bucks. His dad makes pots and pots
of money in securities—but let's
not hear me griping at the rich while wearing
one of my two two-hundred-dollar suits.

Mark draws from a knapsack the books he's bought—
Pound, Lawrence, Durrell (I though he was out),
Smart and Clare (safer choices, both being mad)
and a surprising, handsome *Rubaiyat.*

Mark asks about my job. He has me twice
repeat my salary, each time bulging his eyes
in sham barefaced amazement. Later, alone
and gleefully free to wage my wars in peace,

I derail a quatrain (striking at that band
of Harvard potters who'd "live off the land"
a summer or two before going on
for M.B.A.'s, just as the parents planned):

"A Book of Verses underneath the Bough,
A Jug of Wine, a Loaf of Bread, and Thou-
sands in the Bank; fleeting though Riches be,
And powerless, They comfort anyhow."

Yes . . . And all at once, summer's nearly through.
I return *Parodies,* a week overdue.
And I'm asked to join the firm, beginning next year,
with four months to decide . . . Oftener now

I linger at work, to watch how the setting sun
at once sharpens and softens the skyline;
sometimes—the better for being rare—the dusk-light's
perfect and, while occupied toy boats twine

the Hudson with long, unraveling wakes,
the sun buffs hundreds of windows, reglazes bricks,
ruddies a plane's belly like a robin's,
and seems to free us from billable time, from stocks

and bonds (both words a pun, ironically,
on hand-fetters), leases, estate taxes, proxy
fights, adverse parties, complainants, claimants,
motions to suppress, to enjoin, to quash, oxy-

moronic lengthy briefs, and the whole courtly game
of claim and counterclaim; seems to say we come
through drudgery to glory . . . Look—down there! Wall
Street's turned to gold at last! And there are some

silver nights of emptied offices, raindrops
washing out the glue on those envelopes
in which memories are sealed and the entire
cleared distances offered up, all the old hopes

intact, as if nothing's been mislaid. This obscure
sense that one's past is safely banked somewhere
finds confirmation each time the recumbent
city, touched by darkness, begins to stir

and with a sufferance that's nearly heartbreaking
undergoes a pane by pane awakening
until just as fresh, as sparklingly replete
as last night, or any night before: *not a thing*

is lost. The frail headlights drift, as white as snow
it's fair to say. I'll leave here soon, for good. I know
"for good" is for the better, in some ways, and know
I'll be ready to leave. Or nearly so.

DAYBREAK

Despite the upward flush, the sky's
kindling from lavender to scarlet,
that first scorched crescent of sun
    lifting from the ocean
still comes as something of a surprise.

The sea, shadowed like the floor
of a forest and matted, apparently,
with a tinder-bed of needles,
    bursts in a moment
with flashfire from horizon to shore.

Inland—meanwhile—the hacked, warning
cry of a rooster sounds, saying,
as unfailingly roosters do: Peril
    is at hand, wake *up,*
wake *up,* this is no ordinary morning!

Now a pause, before the rooster's cry
incites another, and another
even fainter, as one by one
    in their loamy dark
they rise and let uprooted voices fly;

quite soon, by the time their wild
several alarm jangles westward
out of hearing's reach, the sea has
    lapsed into smoldering
patches of fire, and the day seems almost mild.

45

The birth of nothing—and yet
  to the world of mathematics it
  was the invention of the wheel.

The Greeks had no symbol
for this strange-traited place-
  keeper; and a millennium would pass

  before an Eastern westward flow,
trade and war, relayed a Hindu
concept of one that's less than one.

  Unadorned it's come down
  in the least prepossessing
of forms, limply evoking

an empty face, a daylight moon,
  the round window of an airplane
  giving onto a cloud . . .

Leibniz, his numbers imbued
with the divine, proposed an ideal
  binary system—wherein His soul

  would be represented
by Ones, Zeroes enclose the void.
We might embellish the metaphor

(let the two shapes lead us further)
and make One a life-kindling
inspired branch of lightning,

Zero a lifeless pond, that pure
    oval of repose before
    the discharging stroke; though it may be

better, truer to the cold beauty
of each to say, "Simply, One is
    the smallest positive whole—and as

    for Zero: more than less than nothing, it
is nothing and precisely that."

BIRCHES

Generously overgrown,
it's still a kind of clearing:
the sunlight's different here
above the fern bed, somehow
brighter and gentler at once
as birches draw the presence
of clouds down into the forest.

While in this light they suggest
(the narrow limbs, and fair skin
peeling as if with sunburn)
something young and feminine,
they will on an afternoon
black with storm evoke that soon-
to-thunder first stroke of lightning.

In composing complements
to the stolid pine, the sun-
siphoning birches vary
not merely with the seasons
but with the minute hourly
unravelings of the day,
freshly hopeful at dawn in their

tattered but immaculate
bandages and at dusk war-
painted, trunks smeared a savage
red; they are becomingly
multiform and a forest

that boasts even a modest
stand of birch maintains its daily

   log of weather conditions
and a hinted timelessness—
as when, given the right light,
birches from their swampy pool
of ferns lift tall saurian
necks to browse, small heads unseen,
in the overhanging leafage.

DUCKWEED

Where there was a pond there's
Now a floating carpet,
  Gold-butter-green,
  And smooth as pond water.
    The carpet shares

With those extensive, spare
Cumulus plains one sees by plane
  A false firmness—
  As if only step lightly
    And it would bear

Your weight; cloud-false, too,
In its suggestion
  Of indwelling light, some
  Deep-deposited radiance.
    Only if you

Kneel to scrutinize
Its surface closely
  Will you begin to see
  How many mini–lily pads
    Of brad's-head size

Were needed to transform
The shadowed pool
  Through emanant domain.
  But dip your hands to part
    The duckweed's warm

Sealing, and here's
A room below: uninviting
   By nature, and one—chill,
   Dim, jumbled—nobody's
      Entered for years.

MINIMS

A Thumbnail Sketch of Unrequited Love

Your lungs expand; you're smitten—
　　She's gnawingly beautiful;

Before long the nail's bitten
　　Right down to the cuticle.

A Möbius Strip

With a minimal twist, the maxim's bent:
There's but one side to every argument.

Bar Song in Winter

When the city's arteries clog with buses,
And the tough stars edge into their niches,
And the light bulbs bloom in all the houses—
　　It's time to fill my glass again.

When the night's still young, but we feel older,
And the tipsy ghosts begin to mutter;
When the snow runs from the coming weather—
　　Please fill up my glass again.

Advice to a Small Child

Don't abandon castles in the sand.
Build them lower, closer to land.

The Integers

They serve as stepping stones, neat
    And fitting niches for the mind's feet—
Over a swamp of roots, oddments, monstrous trailing
    Irrationals that never repeat.

−1 (Negative One)

Depart from the party, one step out the door,
And voices behind sound brighter than before.

−2 (Negative Two)

This couple's linked by lacks, a marriage of
Joint non-interests and the want of love.

Such a Frightening Affair

They've shared now, face to face,
 Maybe a dozen beds—
And still their knees knock heads
 When they embrace.

Trauma

You will carry this suture
 Into the future.
The past never passes.
 It simply amasses.

IN A MUSEUM: FOSSILIZED RAINDROPS

Longer necked than the giraffe,
the air-born creature that left these tracks.

Versicolored, pristine, to which
the chameleon's skin

is rangeless, the swan unclean—
this one's a sun-cowed, cloudy-headed beast

with a spelunker's thirst
for the deepmost narrowing fissure.

Indigene of a sere cirrus
country, and of oppressive ocean cellars

where light never sweeps
and the whole rolling land between,

this amphibian-plus, more wondrous
than the chimera, confirms

through omnipresence its rarity;
one sees finally

this is earth's nonpareil
undiluted animal, the one never bent

by evolution. Time cannot change
  its strict volatility; it retains

  its taste for the rock's
underside and the spouting moment, for paradox—

even down to its descending gurgled
  whisper born in thunder.

DEAD ELMS BY A RIVER

In early spring, unlike the others,
These retain their same shapes, same
Sharp angular lines, edges
Thick with splinters. Dozens
Of shallow snow-fed rivulets sift
Through old dumps of vegetation,
Down toward the river, until the sopping
Banks spill over and the elms stand
With bases under a frigid inch of water.

On all the other trees
Buds cling to the slender branches,
Each a green dot no bigger
Than a bubble of air, and adhering
Just as lightly. Birds—unseen,
Perceived as sweet, disembodied voices—
Call through the blue chilly sky;
And callers echo from distant stations,
These fibrous cries encircling,

Encircling like the shrubs and ferns
That will close upon the elms,
Green infant fists battling
For vacant places. Blind
To light and heat, the elms
Will keep to their winter selves;
A dry company, among the summer foliage
These same gray trunks
Will glimmer, pale as ghosts.

Or nearly the same: gradually,
Far slower than losses of leaves
In a single season, the brittle
Outer branches are torn,
Stripped by wind and rain to contours
Still more spare. The river-wind
Pours through the trees, peeling
Back their bark: underneath,
They are smooth, close-grained columns.

Until later in the summer when one
Is found on the morning after a storm
Snapped like a matchstick and lying
Tossed into the river, it is apt to seem
That with every lost branch the elms
Constrict around an essence hard as crystal,
That under their ash-colored skins
Airless hearts grow more and more indurate:
Core of diamond, core of ice.

The road abruptly changed to dirt,
Thinned until grasses brushed
The car on both sides, and then
Ended in a loop before the marsh.
We hiked along an arm of land held
Firm by cedars, the lake breaking
Like an ocean on one side,
The rippling, flooded wetlands wide
As a lake on the other.
You found a broad white feather
That could perhaps have been
Converted into a serviceable pen;
We searched for precious stones.
Ahead, brown and white shorebirds,
Probably sandpipers, fled from us
Calling with small chipped voices;
So quick, their matchstick legs
Blurred, like hummingbird wings;
And when they finally stopped,
Their low bodies faded wholly
Into the brown and white rocks.
Later, where the cedars clung
Tight against the lake and crowded out
Our path, we turned toward the marsh,
And some rummaging ducks
Scooted raucously away from us,
Wings striking water repeatedly—
Like a stone sent skipping across—
Before they broke with sudden grace
Into the air. We could hear

Waves falling as we wandered
Through woods that held no breeze,
To a small, harsh clearing where
Three or four fallen trees
Crossed in a tangle. We paused there,
In the sun, and something scary slid
As if across the surface of my eye:
Snakes! Among the logs, we began
To pick them out: fat overlapping coils
Lolling in the light, skin
The color of sticks; they were hard
To detect, except when in movement.

Along the lake, where a path had slowly
Collapsed the few feet down
To the shore, up-ending little trees until
Their branches tilted into the water,
We found the body of a doe.
The place was quiet, a pond-sized cove
Where the low waves broke slowly,
Lapping up against the body.
Sand had slipped around the legs,
Blanketing the hard hooves,
But trunk and face lay bare, soft,
The tongue limp and gray beneath
Tiny crooked teeth. A wet eyelash, left
Over an eye picked clean to the bone,
Seemed a tawdry, artificial touch.
I looked for bullets, but found no holes,
Blood, nothing. The massive body lay

Fetid and undisturbed, like a mariner's
Daydream beached up in a storm:
A strange tawny sea-creature . . .
I fanned away the flies that speckled
The blond flank, and we saw them hover,
Land, and then resume their tracking.
We held hands, kneeling beside the body
As if we could impart a gift
Of movement: possible here, on a day
When we'd seen sticks slither
And stones take flight, for this
Animal to rise at our whispering and shake
Sleep from its sandy coat. We watched
The clear waves curl, then break
Against the chest like a heartbeat.

OLD HAT

It was like you, so considerate a man,
to have your papers in order, to leave
your belongings neat; while compelled to grieve,
we were spared the hard, niggling tasks that can
clutter and spoil grief. Yet not even you
understood how a mere cap on its hook,
companion on those outings you still took,
would hang so heavily now for those who,

like you, would keep a tidy house. We've tried
to sort your things, but where are we to hide
those in which some living threads remain?
What we want is to store such things outside
the slow, spiraling loss of love and pain
that turns you, day by day, into a stranger.

THE GHOST OF A GHOST

The pleasures I took from life
were simple things—to play catch
in the evenings with my son,
or tease my daughter (whom I addressed
as Princess Pea), or to watch
television, curled on the floor.
Sometimes I liked to drink too much,
but not too often. Perhaps best
of all was the delight I found
waking to a drowse at one
or two at night and my wife
huffing (soft, not quite a snore)
beside me, a comforting sound.

We had our problems of course,
Emily and I, occasions when
things got out of hand. —Once she threw
a juice glass at me that broke
on the wall (that night I drew
a face there, a clownish man
catching it square on the nose,
and Emily laughed till she cried).
It's true I threatened divorce
a few times (she did too), but those
were ploys, harmless because love ran
through every word we spoke—
and then, an accident, I died.

II

Afterwards, my kids began
having nightmares—when they slept
at all; Emily moved in a haze,
looking older, ruined now, and wept
often and without warning.
The rooms had changed, become mere
photographs in which my face
was oddly missing . . . That first year
without me: summer twilight, and those
long leaf-raking Saturdays
without me, and Christmas morning—
the following August a new man,
a stranger, moved in and took my place.

You could scarcely start to comprehend
how queer it is, to have your touch
go unfelt, your cries unheard
by your family. Princess!—I called—
Don't let that stranger take your hand!
And—*Em, dear, love, he has no right
to you.*
       Where did they think I'd gone?
who walked the house all day, all night,
all night. It was far too much
for anyone to endure, and,
hammered by grief one ugly dawn,
I broke. I am still here!—I bawled
from the den—Still here! And no one stirred.

But in time I learned a vicious trick,
a way of gently positing
a breath upon a person's neck
to send an icy run of fear
scampering up the spine—anything,
anything to show them who was near!
. . . Anything, but only to retrieve
some sense that nothing is more
lasting than the love built week by week
for years; I had to believe
again that these were people I'd
give everything, even a life, for.
Then—a second time, and slow—I died.

III

Now I am a shadow of my
former shadow. Seepage of a kind
sets in. Settled concentrations thin.
Amenably—like the smile become
a pond, the pond a mud-lined
bed, from which stems push, pry
and hoist aloft seed-pods that
crack into a sort of grin—
things come almost but not quite
full circle; within the slow
tide of years, water dilutes to light,
light to a distant, eddying hum . . .
In another time, long ago,

I longed for a time when I'd
still felt near enough to recall
the downy scrape of a peach skin
on my tongue, the smell of the sea,
the pull of something resinous.
By turns, I have grown other-wise.
I move with a drift, a drowse that roams
not toward sleep but a clarity
of broadened linkages; it's in
a state wholly too gratified
and patient to be called eagerness
that I submit to a course which homes
outward, and misses nothing at all.

A MICHIGAN GHOSTTOWN

It's as though even the ghosts
Have left: no sense of anyone
Lingering here; nothing to weight
The hundreds of poplars—locally
"Popple"—flickering in the light
Breezing of this cool Superior
Noon. Had I not been told
Where to pick out the vined
Roots of a settlement, I might
Have seen no trace at all.

                     It was nothing
But a boomtown, a roof
And a drink, built to last
As long as the timber did, which
Wasn't long. Yet the buzzsaws spun
Mounds and mounds of gold
Dust before they were done.

Up here, back then, it was boom-and-bust;
And after the bust
Sixty, seventy years of thin
Northern sun, of fog turning to snow,
And a tentative, tendrilous
Scrapping with rock and ice,
A re-routing of roots,
A noiseless supplanting as
The popple moved back in—

Trees take the streets.

ANGEL

There between the riverbank
and half-submerged tree trunk
it's a kind of alleyway
inviting loiterers—
    in this case, water striders.

Their legs, twice body-length, dent
the surface, but why they don't
sink is a transparent riddle:
the springs of their trampoline
    are nowhere to be seen.

Inches and yet far below, thin
as compass needles, almost, min-
nows flicker through the sun's
tattered netting, circling past
    each other as if lost.

Enter an angel, in
the form of a dragon-
fly, an apparition whose
coloring, were it not real,
    would scarcely be possible:

see him, like a sparkler,
tossing lights upon the water,
surplus greens, reds, milky
blues, and violets blended
    with ebony. Suspended

like a conductor's baton,
he hovers, then goes the one
way no minnow points: straight
up, into that vast solution
of which he's a concentrate.

A ROCK WITH A VIEW

MAZATLÁN, MEXICO

Though just a ship as it drags
from the harbor, a change
takes place on the open sea.
With distance its speed declines,
or seems to gradually,
until bit by bit it lags
to a sunny spot and stands still.
Gray and red, what a strange
island it makes!—with its flags
now blooms, pipes and ladders vines,
and smokestack a volcanic hill.

The hill behind me teems
with like abundance: mat
of vegetation plaited
over mat, until it seems
no growth could erupt from that,
and yet the cacti do.
Glabrous, fat, they look inflated,
like balloons, except where
vines have swarmed into the air
to cover the cacti, too,
and tree-impostors are created.

Lava-like, in turgid waves
from the hilltop, this warm flow
of heavy leafage spills
as if to drown the bay below—
yet never reaches the shore.
The deadly salt air drills

its holes, burns all leaves before
they find the sea; the hill's
green gives way to tumbled stone,
like a row of upthrust graves,
salt-crust edges white as bone.

From a slumped hillside, a ragged
border of greenery
trailing blackened vines,
then piles of cracked boulders
on which the sun shines
brokenly, and an unsteady sea,
waves toppling at the shoulders
to sprawl flat among debris—
no edge that is not jagged,
in all the splintered scenery
no direct, simple lines.

. . . Lines both sweeping and clear
are found where the ocean
is gently veined: the freighter,
whose sides (though they fence
a swamp of pipes) are sheer;
and beyond, so much greater
the assimilating eye
must now admit the immense
freighter as a toy, the horizon—
that seam of sea and sky
which is the toy ship's destination.

A NOTE ABOUT THE AUTHOR

Brad Leithauser was born in Michigan in 1953 and grew up there. He attended Cranbrook School for Boys, Harvard College—where he twice received the Garrison Prize for best poetry by an undergraduate and twice the Academy of American Poets Prize—and Harvard Law School. His poems and reviews have appeared in a large number of magazines and periodicals, among them the *New Republic*, the *New Yorker*, the *Atlantic Monthly*, and the *Washington Post*.

Since 1980, he and his wife, the poet Mary Jo Salter, have lived in Japan, where he is a Research Fellow at the Kyoto Comparative Law Center. He is the Amy Lowell Poetry Traveling Scholar for 1981–82.

A NOTE ON THE TYPE

The text of this book was set in film in a typeface called Griffo, a camera version of Bembo, the well-known monotype face. The original cutting of Bembo was made by Francesco Griffo of Bologna only a few years after Columbus discovered America. It was named for Pietro Bembo, the celebrated Renaissance writer and humanist scholar who was made a cardinal and served as secretary to Pope Leo X. Sturdy, well-balanced, and finely proportioned, Bembo is a face of rare beauty. It is, at the same time, extremely legible in all of its sizes.

Composition by Superior Printing, Champaign, Illinois

Printed by American Book–Stratford Press, Inc.,
Saddle Brook, New Jersey

Designed by Joe Marc Freedman